LOOK, BREATHE

LOOK, BREATHE

POEMS & TRANSLATIONS

CHRIS POWICI

& FRIENDS

RED SQUIRREL PRESS

First published in 2022 by Red Squirrel Press
36 Elphinstone Crescent
Biggar
South Lanarkshire
ML12 6GU
www.redsquirrelpress.com

Layout, design and typesetting by Gerry Cambridge
e:gerry.cambridge@btinternet.com

Cover photograph: Wing of *Sympetrum striolatum*
Copyright © Gerry Cambridge

A CIP catalogue record for this book is available from the
British Library.

ISBN: 978 1 913632 31 1

Red Squirrel Press is committed to a sustainable future.
This publication is printed in the UK by Imprint Digital
using Forest Stewardship Council certified paper.
www.digital.imprint.co.uk

Contents

Preface

In the autumn of 2019, I asked my friend the novelist and poet Kevin MacNeil, if he'd like to translate a poem of mine into his native Gaelic. I had an idea that both versions would make good neighbours on the pages of a Scottish literary magazine. Kevin said yes right way (he's that kind of guy) and I joked that, being such a slow writer, if I could find translators for all my poems, I'd only have to write half of my next collection.

Over the following days and weeks, the joke turned serious. I may only speak English but by including translations in a collection I could say something about my family history and where I find myself in the world. The first languages of friends and family include Scots, Gaelic, Romanian, Italian, Flemish and a host of others. Scotland itself, like so many countries, has opened its doors to languages from all around the globe, whether through immigration or by dint of the myriad ways that the literatures of the world tend to treat borders as crossing points rather than barriers.

Then another truth hit home. My poetry likes to look at places where the so-called human and natural worlds overlap, riverbanks, shorelines, field, paths, woods, roadside verges etc. In other words, I try to notice stuff and, if I pay attention well, say something about how my life fits, or sometimes doesn't fit, with all those other lives happening around me. But maybe, if my poems could find new ways of speaking, they could say different things. After all, a feeling *for* the earth—for what it has to offer us physically, spiritually and emotionally—may be a universal human trait, but how the earth itself touches our senses and enters our thinking varies according to geography and history, culture and language. That's why so many of the poems in this book are as much translocations as they are translations. I may not understand every word and phrase, but their sounds and textures speak to the heart as well as the ear. Thanks to the generosity, insight and sheer artistry of the many people who've contributed to *Look, Breathe* their versions of my poems have ridden a sense of fellow-feeling to places I could never have imagined. What's more, they make fine neighbours.

Chris Powici
January 2022

Argaty

half a winter moon, a low hill
trees on the ridge

birch branches shine with an hour ago's rain
and I swear that dink of light
high beyond the sheep fields
is far-flung Mars, wanting me to look

deep February night, no streetlamps
so cold my breath rises in thin, pale clouds
and everything wants me to look

a moon, a wood, rainwater, wet bark
stars blinking on twigs

Argaty

hauf a winter mune, a laigh brae
trees on the rig

birk branches glintin wi the rain
o a hauf-oor syne

an I sweir thon blink o licht
heigh ayont the sheep-fields
is hyne-awa Mars, wantin me tae luik

deep Februar nicht, nae street-lichts
—that cauld ma braith sclims
in shilpit cloods
an a'thin's wantin me tae luik

a mune, a shaw, rainwatter,
weet bark o trees
sternies blinterin oan twigs

Drystone

another winter's ice and rain
the drub and scrape of hoof and horn
and these last lichen-riddled slabs
could creak and drop
to the bare, wet moor

but not yet

they stand and cling, they lean
against the blue May sky
the bright wind

a wheatear whistles from its granite nook
and a blackface ewe
pushes through the swaying broom
rubs her tatty arse against this poor, half-fallen dyke
and offers up a bleat or two
in praise of stone

Dryston

aniddir winter's frost an faa
da scratch an scrummel o hoof an horn
an dese hidmaest lichened slabs
could girn an drap
tae da weet, nekkit hill

but no yit

dey staund an cling, dey lean
agin da blue May lift
da bricht blaa

a wheatear whisltles fae hit's granite neuk
an a blackfiss yow
shivs trow da swayin broom
elts hir clerty erse agin dis puir amos, half faan daek
an offers up a böl or twa
in praise o ston

Claonaig Ferry

—Oh I feel that you are near me, Oh I wish it to be
                                        The Unthanks

I lean against the wet steel of the guardrail
listen to the engine's soft, oily breath
and creak of tarpaulin from the car deck

a gannet glides through drifts of summer rain
a cormorant stands for a second
on a green wave
and shakes the sea from its wings

halfway to Claonaig
we're all of us getting by
on weather and oil and light

guillemot bob on the swell

just below the surface
moon jellies billow and sway

Claonaig Ferry

> —*Oh I feel that you are near me, Oh I wish it to be*
> The Unthanks

Leanin tae the railins' drookit steel
I dirl til the diesel's ily souch
an the reishle o tarps frae the car deck.

A solan snooves through simmer smirr
a scart stauns up on a green wave
jist for a second
tae shak the sea frae its wings.

Hauf owre tae Claonaig
we're hingin-in thegither
amang the licht, the ile, an the weather

maggies are oot on the swall

i the cauldrife watter
the jeely fish wax and swyve

Coastal Town

a big October moon rises from the deep bay
shows its hurt, radiant face to the first stars
and a whooper swan looking to land

down here, just the earth up to its usual tricks—

a sea wind, an autumn tide swaying
the bladderwrack on a spit of beach;
the glad serious faces of boys
leaning on the bike-park wall

a woman watches a herring gull
flap and cry from the kirk roof
opens an old door, goes inside

afterwards, only the seaweed-scented air
streetlamps like small wet moons
some boys, somewhere, laughing
bike wheels spinning in the dusk

Costal Toon

a grett October mön buts fae de djub o de voe
shaas its skammit, sheenin fiss tae de foremist starns
an a whooper swaan skoitin fir a laandin

doon here, joost de aert up tae its öswil klooks—

a bakflan, a hairst string swittlin
de bratwaar apo a sheave o saand;
de blyde sair faces o bouys
heeldin apo de bike-park daek

a wife waaks a skorie
flaag an greet fae de kirk röf
oppins an aald door, gings inbi,

eftir, joost de tang-waff air
kloss-lamps lik peerie weet möns
some bouys, ee pliss, gaffin
bike wheels spinnin i de darkenin

Guest House

October sunlight fills
the green curtains.

On the bedside table
these bright coins, a brass key.

The thought of you, now,
is like a leaf on a river.

Gæstehus

Efterårssol fylder
de blågrønne gardiner.

På natbordet
de blanke mønter, en nøgle af messing.

Tanken om dig nu
er som et blad på åen.

Falls

clamour of eddies and foam-edged
kinks of bright November water sliding
over pine roots and half-drowned rock

so many flashes and glints
so many cold quick voices

but lean into the breeze
take a breath, listen close—
all the river says
is how to let go
how to fall

just a noise among trees
it's all grace notes and throwaway riffs
a thing of rain and stone
making itself up as it goes along

Eas

gleo guairneán agus caisirníní
le ciumhais cúráin
uisce na samhna gile
ag sleamhnú thar fhréamhacha giúise
agus thar charraigeacha leath báite

an oiread splanc agus drithle
an oiread guth fuar agus tapaidh

ach lig do thaca leis an bhfeothan
glac anáil, éist go dlúth—
ní deir an abhainn
ach conas ligean as
conas titim anuas

díreach fothram ar fud na gcrann
díreach maisiú agus rifeanna caite i dtraipisí
rud as báisteach agus cloch
á chumadh féin is é ag gabháil an bealach

The Wild Summer

i.m. Angus Dunn

Nights and days of blinding rain, Atlantic lows
sweeping across the carse
trees and hills lost in thick noonday mist.

Now this raw light
and a hard Steppe wind pouring down Glen Tye
towards the late sun.

A raven lifts from a fencepost
and gives itself to the cold, marvellous air
pitching and wheeling
as if there's no tomorrow, as if there's
only ever hunger, longing, flight—here, now

and this, as you know, is the real poem Angus—
a lone dark bird telling the truth about the world
telling it well—
not these words

though, given time, I'll get them as right as I can
even if there's no raven, just skeins of autumn greylag
flowing calmly south.

Even if it's way too late by then.

Snell Simmer

i.m. Angus Dunn

Watherfu'days. Daudin shours.
Pouskins scoorin the Carse.
Wid an brae dernt in haar.

An noo this whitit licht, as wastlins
thin faur-easterlies smoor Glentye.

A corbie heezes frae a stob,
gies itsel tae the snell, byordnar air
birlin, joukin; mindin us,
aiblins, there's naethin but now, naethin but
hunger an greenin, naethin ahent the toom lift.

Ach, Angus, this here's the leed, the richt leed,
weel ye ken: this lane corbie scrievin'
the trowthfu things—no these words, mind,
no my words, but the perfit words.

Ach, gied time, A'll ding them bonnie as A can;
nae corbie for me, jist straigles o stibble-geese
beatin the soothwarts seelence.

Jist gie us time;
tho weel A ken, it's time we're wantin.

Gorse

We have watched peewit flap and glide
over the bright, sheep-trodden fields
the fierce yellow gorse spill
over the broken backs of drystane walls—
and we have come home to TV news
that twenty-two people have died in a care home in Paisley.
That's twenty-two ways to walk in the rain
or glance at the moon
or nudge a lover awake
gone for good behind closed doors
behind ordinary, quiet, terrible doors

but we don't have a word for it yet—
this strange, new hurt—
we don't have a name
so we think, we need to think
about peewit scattering
their high, reedy cries on a soft wind
about the wild April gorse
how it rises and blooms.

Gorse

Wir watcht a peewit flott an flap
ower da bricht yow bruckit hill
da veeve yalloo gorse spill
ower maracled rigs o dry ston waas—
an wir come hom tae news on da telly.
A score an twa deid in a care hom in Paisley.
Jun's a score an twa wyes tae wakk i da rain
or eye da mön
or wakk a sleepin lover
gien fur ay ahint closed doors
ahint quiet, gluffsome doors

but we haenna ony wird fur hit yit—
dis unkan ache—
we haenna a nem
so we think, we *maun* think
aboot peewit shooin
dir high reedy cries on a saft wind
aboot da wild April gorse
fu hit rises an blooms.

The Quick Rain

A roe deer lies cradled in the crook of your arms
a buck of a few months, maybe a year.
Its ribs press against your ribs
its neck touches your neck
but no muscle twitch, no heave of breath

You just want to do the right thing—
lay the body down among the grasses
and clovers at the side of the road
but it's a rainy October night, without moon or stars
and for all you know, the grass could be tangled
in brambles and fence-wire
and the weight of the deer in your arms
could be the weight of your soul in the world.
For all you know.

Its hooves dangle and swing
and the quick rain beats against the skin and eyes
like a wild clock.

An t-Uisge Luath

Tha boc-earb na laighe ann an creathail do ghàirdeanan,
earbag nach eil ach beagan mìosan a dh' aois, neo bliadhna
's dòcha. Tha aiseanan a' beantainn ri d' aiseanan,
tha amhach a' beantainn ri d' amhach; ach chan eil fhèitheag
a' snaothadh, chan eil e a' tarraing anail ann.

Tha thu dìreach airson an rud ceart a dhèanamh—
an corp a chur sìos anns an fheòir agus 'sa chlòbhair
ri taobh an rathaid, ach 's e oidhche fhliuch 'san Dàmhair a th' ann,
gun ghealach 's gun rionnagan, agus cho fad 's a 's aithne dhut,
dh' fhaodadh an fheòir a bhith air a dhol na paidearan
le dris is uèir feansa, agus dh' fhaodadh nach eil ann an cudthrom
na h-earbaig nad ghàirdeanan ach cudthrom
d' anma anns an t-saoghail. Cho fad 's a 's aithne dhut.

Tha ìngnean ag udalach, a' luasgadh,
agus tha an t-uisge luath a' bualadh
air a' chraiceann 's air a shùilean
mar ghleog fhiadhaich.

Nights Like These

Is it all the same thing—
an autumn wind blowing
through the bracken of the lane
fox bark, twig crack
rain in the trees—
the same wild amen
in darkness being spoken?

Dit Soort Nachten

Is het allemaal hetzelfde—
een herfstwind die waait
doorheen de varens langs de weg
een vos die blaft, een tak die kraakt
regen in de bomen—
hetzelfde wilde einde
uitgesproken in het donker?

A Field in February

No fat-bellied ewes flinch and scatter
no Angus cow lifts her slow head from the good earth
looking and chewing. All that's weeks away.
Just grass, frost, a few oaks yet to leaf
and a daub of shadow, a shiver of wings
—kestrel or peregrine—under the pale sun.

So you lean on the gate
and watch a bird, whatever its name,
scour the bare, bright field
for rabbit tracks, pigeon feathers
glints of blood or skin—every rut, every stone—
until the sun has fallen low among the trees
the trees look black and sacred
in the late winter light
and hunger and seeing are the same thing.

A Field in February

No fat yowes tae skail oot, fleggid
no Angus coo tae lift her heid slow fae the good grund
lukkan an chowan. That's a piece awey yet.
Chist gress, frost, twathree low willow, a grey sea ahint
an a dab o shadow, a pivver o weengs
—moosie-haak or catabelly?—under a wersy sun.

Furtiver. You lean on the gett
an watch the bird quaarteran the bare, bright field
for a fleester o voldro, a stirleen fendan
a glisk o bluid or skin—every dreel, every stone—
till the sun's geen doon on the sea
tae a blink o gold at the aidge
in the winter grimleens
an you're hungry an thinkan long for the light.

At Sheriffmuir

all day this thick summer rain
no sun to speak of
only the moor dimmed down
to a brown, heathery blur

a ewe trots through the heavy grass
and stands at the edge of a peat hag
so drenched, so calm
she could be breathing rain
at any moment she could become rain

her fleece is turning into water
her eyes are wet and black and deep

the roadside bracken shivers
under its hood of glints
and the blue harebell petals bend
and give, a little,
as if they know there's more to come

there's always more to come

the same rain seeps into the dark tangle of your hair
makes its slow way down the skin at the back of your neck
cool and silent, but telling you something
about here and now and how close the world is—
grass, bracken, a few small damp flowers
all it takes to start seeing things again
to begin

At Sheriffmuir

aa day, dingin simmer rain
nae sun tae spik o
jist the muir drummelt doon
tae a broon, heatherie loom

a yowe lowps throu the swarra girse
syne staans on the lip o a peat hag
sappin, serene
she could be wauchtin rain
ony meenit noo she could bi rain itsel

her fleesh is thawin tae watter
her een are weet an black an deep

the brechan bi the road shithers
anaith its hood o glintin dreep
an the blaewart petals coorie
doon, a bittie,
as if they ken ere's mair tae come

ere's aywis mair tae come

the verra rain sypes intae the derk raivel o yer hair
maks its slow wye doon the skin o yer naver
caul an quyet, but kythin ye summin
aboot here an noo an hoo nearhan the warld is—
girse, brechan, a wee curn o weet flooers
aa it taks tae start takkin tent again
tae begin

Bracklinn Woods

—October 2020

twig-rip and bark-clatter
of leaves in their thousands—
birch, beech, oak
black-riddled yellows
bruised-orange greens—
blowing sideways through
the shook trees
the thrash and yell of it
the shattered singing
as if they couldn't give a toss
for peace or anything
but this broken sunlight
brilliant wind

Bracklinn Wid

—back-end 2020

bark-brattle
the shidder
o leaf upon leaf bladdit—beech, birk, aik
yellaes sclacht in black, greens hawn in orange
blawn endlang in shakit Keltie treen
the scoorit chirm, a bowsterous bawl
nae heed tae cark for ony lee, forby
this brichtenin
this beelin blaw

A Lanarkshire Field

11am December sun
lighting the bare green hills

birch trees, a quick river
frost on the bracken and fence-wire

and muddy-hooved sheep bowing
their neat busy heads
to the bright cold grass
as if nothing else matters
nothing else shines

ITALIAN TRANSLATION BY ELISABETTA TORENO

Un campo nel Lanarkshire

Sono le 11.00, e il sole di Dicembre
illumina le nude colline verdi

Giù, betulle, un corso d'acqua celere,
brina sulla felce e sui fili, ferrosi,
delle recinzioni

Le pecore, i loro zoccoli infangati,
inchinano le loro teste immacolate e intente
verso l'erba fredda e fulgida
perché nient'altro conta
nient'altro rifulge

Fathoms

—Arran, July 2018

The patio gates of the Mara Fish Bar & Deli
have been carved into the bodies of otters
flirting with one another in a slow, wild dance.
The patio railings are blue wood.
Beyond them, the warm tarmac of the Shore Road
a slither of beach
and thirty yards out to sea that lump of wet grey rock
where Marvin Elliott's sculpted seal rests in the sun.
The Atlantic splashes whitely over its dark back
and a herring gull hangs nonchalantly
over cool summer waves
those shining fathoms
where my soul has gone for a swim.

Fathoms

—Arran, July 2018

The yetts o the Mara Café & Deli
are collit intae the like o otters
tovin wi yin anither in a slaw
an gallus dance.
The patio railings are blue wid.
Ayont them, the leepit tarmac o the Shore Road,
a slester o strand,
an thritty yairds oot tae sea
yon daud o grim weet rock
whaur Marvin Elliott's sculptit seal
ligs in the sun.
The Atlantic jaups whitely
 ower its dooth back
an a willie gou hings nonchalantly
ower cuilie simmer waws,
those glentin fathoms
whaur my soul gans for douks.

Glen Tye

how we manage to raise ourselves
into the delicate dawn
—Angus Dunn

some day I'll raise myself
into a dawn so delicate
I won't have to say anything
not a word
just look, breathe—

whaleback hills, a dripping sky
birch trees and drystone walls fall away
a raven takes shape in the rain

Glen Tye

how we manage to raise ourselves
into the delicate dawn
— Angus Dunn

sune enuch Ah'll raise masel
intae a dawn sae delicate
Ah'll haud ma wheesht

jist luik, breathe—

whaleback hills, a dreich-day sky
birks n drystane dykes tummel awa
a corbie taks shape in the drizzlin smirr

April

—i.m. Helen Lamb

These things are happening now:

an April wind
rook nests swaying in the trees like dark bells
the thought of her, in the garden, watching.

Ferns tremble by the shed door.
Last night's rain drips from the firethorn leaves.

All this brilliant shock of world
and the thought of her watching.

Everything now.

Aprilie

—în memoria lui Helen Lamb

Aceste lucruri se întâmplă acum:

vânt de aprilie
cuiburi de corbi legănate în copaci ca niște clopote întunecate
gânduri despre ea, în grădină, privind.

Ferigi tremură lângă ușa șopronului.
Ploaia de aseară picură de pe frunzele de piracanta.

Tot acest șoc sclipitor peste lume
si gândul la ea privind.

E totul acum.

The God of Rain

I know you

your loose black hair
your face like a pool brimming
with leaves and the shadows of leaves

the cool well of your mouth
that way you have of speaking
in many restless, echoey tongues

bog cotton, deergrass, a peewit feather
caught in fence-wire—
when you fall, you fall from grace
into more grace

and when it all gets too much—
your wet-petal glow
your sea-scented breath—
when we must be alone
with our hurt and our luck
you hide in the trees like a moth

Maleya Devaru

nā ninna balle

bicchida ninna karigūdalu
tumbida koḷadante ninna moga
elegaḷu elegaḷa neraḷu

ninna bāyi tampu bāvi
ninna mātina pari
ashānthiya marudhvanigaḷu

būralu hatti, nīḷa niluva hullu, ṭiṭṭiba gari
muḷḷu beliyali sikkikonḍante—
bīḷuvāga nīnu bīḷuve anugrahadinda
innashṭu anugrahakke

mattidellā mīridāga—
ninna toida daḷada kānti
ninna usiru kaḍalina gandha—
ontiyādāga nāvu
namma novu adhrashṭadondige
maradalli nīnu kēṭadante aḍaguve

Happens

The Higgs Boson is estimated…to travel less than a billionth of an inch between when it's produced and when it decays.
—Sean Carroll, *The Particle at the End of the Universe*

Grandparents' voices uninterruptedly talking, in Eternity
—Elizabeth Bishop, 'The Moose'

things happen

a bus moves slowly on a forest road
some thin mist, night coming on
the passengers talk about grandchildren
and weather and who's died
and who's still with us by the grace of God

a woman leans her head against the window
a moose steps from the trees

or in the Large Hadron Collider at CERN
in proton collisions glowing on a screen
the merest hint of the merest shiver
of everything there is

for a moment, the world looks back at us
fathomable, real

the trembling of a particle
a moose, moonlit and still, at the edge of a wood—
things happen and are held
and are gone

Skaes

The Higgs Boson is estimated...to travel less than a billionth
of an inch between when it's produced and when it decays.
—Sean Carroll, *The Particle at the End of the Universe*

Grandparents' voices uninterruptedly talking, in Eternity
—Elizabeth Bishop, 'The Moose'

tings skae

a bus gings langsome alang a widdi-rodd
daalamist, de draa o hömin
de passengers spik o oys
an wadder an dem at's awaa
an wha's still wi wis bi de grace o Him Abön

a wife heelds her haed fornenst de windoo
a müs stramps fae de widdis

or i de Large Hadron Collider at CERN
i de glöd o proton dusts apo a screen
de peeriest skaar o de mootiest gludder
o aa dat is

fir a start, de warld kans wis back
faddomable, real

de dirlin o a hirni
a moose, mönlit an kjeppit, at de lip o a wood—
tings skae an ir hadden
an ir wan

everything is touch and go
communion and decay

and we're left with—what exactly?

in a white vase on a mahogany table
the tulips are beginning to die

rainy April light fills the dining room window

somewhere a bird long asleep
sings its blue awakening

aa is evalous
communion an kassen

an we're left wi—whit, noo?

i de white vase apo de mahogany table
de tulips ir faan upon

de ben-end windoo is lipperin wi weety April licht

sumwye a bird lang blinnd
is sheerlin its blue-litt waaknin

The Old Life

—i.m. Helen Lamb

A mile up the sheep track and I almost pray
you're seeing these gorse flowers shake in the blowing sleet
the noon sun rip through thin Atlantic cloud
and the Minch tide fall, bright and hungry, on Achmelvich beach
but even if I could get death to shift its weight
I've a hunch your glance would drift
from this cold stramash of wind and light
to a terraced house in a Perthshire lane—
a varnished sill, tulips in a white jug,
and through the kitchen window
that patch of damp spring grass
where you'd lean a rake into a litter of moss and elder leaves
and watch the come and go of blue tits to the hazel
at home in the old life of grace and habit
those mild, right-as-rain afternoons.

An t-Sean Bheatha

—i.m. Helen Lamb

Mìle suas rathad nan caorach cha mhòr nach eil mi ag ùrnaigh
gu faic thu blàth a' chonaisg a' luasgadh san fhlin,
grian meadhan an latha a' reubadh neòil tan' a' Chuain Shiar
agus làn a' Chuain Sgìth tuiteam, glan 's acrach, air Achadh Mhealbhaich
ach fiù 's nan toirinn air a' bhàs an cuideam a th' ann a shioftadh
tha car de bheachd agam gum biodh do shùil a' drioftadh
on stramais-sa de ghaoith 's de sholais spealgta
gu taigh barraideach na lànaige an Siorrachd Pheairt
sòla slìobaichte, tuiliopan—ann an siuga ghil—
tro uinneig a' chidsin bad de dh' fheur fhliuich Earraich,
an ràc ann an grunnd chòinnich 's duilleagan dromain
's tu coimhead tilleadh 's teicheadh nan cailleachagan don challtainn,
aig an taigh anns an t-sean bheatha de ghràis 's ghnàthais,
na feasgairean caoin ud, 's iad cho ceart sa ghabhas.

Lamlash Night

—looking out to Holy Isle, August 2016

gulls put their faith in café roofs
and car park walls
even the little iron-coloured waves
where they drift, half-asleep

their brisk rufflings
their twitches and murmurs
are ways the night has found
to talk to itself
carelessly, on and on

just offshore, a wet glimmer
of hawsers and chains

pull hard enough and I'll haul in a ketch
maybe the island ferry will slide up the beach
and a boatload of monks tumble over the pebbles
gleaming and bald as fish

maybe

meanwhile the chitter of gulls
the push of the tide

everything's as ordinary and holy as bread or rain
as the way I remember my mother's hand on my sleeve
pale, liver-spotted, so thin
it seemed no more than the weight of a glove

Lamlash Night

—looking out to Holy Isle, August 2016

gulls pit thur faith in dookits
an car park waws
an thi wee iron-colourt waves
where they doze, half-driftin

thur brisk rufflins
thur twitches an murmurs
ur wiys thi night's found oot
how tae talk tae itsel
careless, oan and oan

jist offshore, a wet glimmer
eh hawsers an chains

pul hard enough an'll haul in a ketch
mibeez thi island ferry ull slide up thi beach
an a boatload eh monks tuml err thi pebbles
gleamin an bald as fish

mibeez

it thi same time thi chitter eh thi gulls
thi push eh thi tide

iverythin's as oardinary an holy as breed an driech
as the wiy a kent ma mam's hand oan ma sleeve
pale, liver-spottit, so thin
it seemed nae mair'n thi weight eh a glove

a few masthead lights blink in the bay

beyond Holy Isle, the moon
—that shining, far-out buoy—
rides the black swell
making sense of the depths

a few mastheed lights blink in thi bay

eftur Holy Isle, thi moon
—that shining, far-oot buoy—
rides thi black swell
maikin sense eh thi depths

Translators and Translations

CATALINA GEORGE

A published Romanian poet and former journalist, Catalina George now lives in the West Midlands and aims to be a published poet in English.

A very concise, ethereal piece, this poem was so easy to translate into Romanian that it almost frightened me I was not doing it properly. It was one of those (rare) instances where the lyricism of simplicity just fell into words. It might have been easier to translate because I knew Helen and I know Chris.

MAGI GIBSON

Magi Gibson is a leading voice in Scottish poetry. She draws inferences from the little things in life (shopping for stationery, admiring a stranger's hat, drinking tea with a friend) that affect the big issues in all our lives—growing older, poverty and loss. Her latest is collection is *I Like Your Hat*, published by Luath.

JOHN GLENDAY

John Glenday's *Selected Poems* were published by Picador in 2020. A pamphlet of poems about the Tay Estuary, *The Firth*, was published by Mariscat Press in the same year. He describes himself as an avid versioner rather than a translator. The Scots word for translate—'owerset' also means to confront and overcome troubles and difficulties which he finds appropriate.

RODY GORMAN

Rody Gorman is an Irish-born poet who lives on the Isle of Skye and whose main creative medium is Scottish Gaelic. He was born in Dublin on 1 January 1960. Rody is editor of *An Guth*, an annual Irish and Scottish Gaelic poetry anthology.

CHARLIE GRACIE

Charlie Gracie is a poet and writer, originally from Baillieston, Glasgow and now living on the edge of the Trossachs. His most recent collection is *Tales from the Dartry Mountains* (Diehard).

KATHLEEN JAMIE

Kathleen Jamie is an award-winning Scottish poet and essayist whose collections include *The Overhaul* and *The Bonniest Companie* (poetry), and *Sightlines* and *Surfacing* (essays). In 2018, Kathleen was elected as a fellow of the Royal Society of Edinburgh and in 2021, Scotland's National Makar.

WILLIAM LETFORD

Billy Letford has two collections of poetry published, *Bevel* and *Dirt*, both with Carcanet Press.

I loved the poem so much I hardly wanted to touch it. So I just imagined speaking it, in my accent, and let the words fall accordingly.

PETER MACKAY

Peter Mackay is a writer, lecturer and broadcaster; his most recent book of poems is *Nàdur De / Some Kind of* (Acair 2020)

Working 'The Old Life' into Gaelic the rhythms and line length pulled it into the form of a loose sonnet, with a relatively regular rhythm. There is a kind of hinge in the middle of the first and last lines where the same sound is repeated or reworked, and through which I hope that some of Chris's wonderful light and lightness might flow…

KEVIN MACNEIL

Kevin MacNeil is a leading Scottish novelist, poet, playwright and screenwriter, born and raised in the Outer Hebrides. His most recent novel, *The Brilliant & Forever*, was shortlisted for the Saltire Fiction Book of the Year Award.

HUGH MCMILLAN
Hugh McMillan has lived all his life in Dumfries and Galloway and has worked to encourage new writing there and an appreciation of its literary heritage. He describes his Scots translation of Fathoms as mid Nithsdale.

ALISON MILLER
Alison Miller was born and grew up in Orkney and has now returned after many years in Glasgow. She writes, reads and lives by the sea.

Translating 'A Field in February' into Orcadian presented challenges beyond finding Orkney words for the English of the poem. There are no oaks to speak of here and very few trees of any stature outside the shelter of the town. It didn't feel Orcadian to include the 'black and sacred trees'. Peregrines too are rarely seen here; raptor food is often voles and ground-nesting birds. (I could have kept the rabbit, but in one of my more spectacular sightings of a male hen harrier, he dropped like a stone from the sky and plucked a starling from a branch of a low sycamore.) You're never far from the sea here. I couldn't replicate the image of the trees as the sun went down. Instead I transported the author/watcher to an Orkney field near the shore, let the sun sink into the sea and hoped there might be a hint of the transcendence in Chris Powici's original poem in my last lines.

Glossary
yowes—ewes
skail oot—scatter
fleggid—frightened
coo—cow
heid—head
lukkan—looking
chowan—chewing
a piece awey—some time away
chist—just

gress—grass
twathree—a few
ahint—behind
pivver—tremble or quiver
moosie-haak—kestrel
catabelly—hen harrier
wersy—weak
furtiver—anyway; whatever
gett—gate
waatch—watch
quaarteran—quartering
fleester—I use this here to suggest a slight rustling movement; its
    dictionary definition is 'a light shower' but in my family it was
    used to signify a mild flap, nerviness, edginess
voldro—vole esp. the Orkney vole, a favourite food of the hen harrier
stirleen—starling, also a favourite hen harrier food
fendan—looking for worms, insects
glisk—glimpse
bluid—blood (pronounced more 'blid' than the Scots version)
dreel—furrow
geen—gone
doon—down
tae a blink o gold—to a glimpse of gold
aidge—edge
grimleens—dusk
thinkan long—longing for

MARIA THERESA MOERMAN IB
Maria Theresa Moerman IB is a Dutch-Danish artist and writer based in Blairgowrie. She is a student on the MFA in Creative Writing at the University of St Andrews.

GEETHA PRABHU
'The God of Rain' was translated into Kannada by Geetha Prabhu, an amateur naturalist and avid photographer who

lives in the city of Mysore in Karnataka, India. The translation was facilitated by her daughter Gayathri Prabhu who was the Charles Wallace India Writing Fellow at the University of Stirling, Scotland, from February to May 2020.

The literary process of negotiating two languages took place on long video calls with Geetha during Gayathri's term at Stirling when the Covid-19 pandemic first broke out in the UK, and the poem's sensibility helped evoke the pathos of rain in two continents. This was Geetha's first attempt at translation and she drew from decades of engagement with Kannada literature. Her intention and effort was in capturing the nuances of the poem, to carry through the poet's vision as closely as possible. Kannada is the official language of the southern state of Karnataka. With around 60 million speakers, Kannada has been accorded classical status by the Government of India and possesses a strong literary and scholarly tradition of over a thousand years.

SHANE STRACHAN

Shane Strachan holds a PhD in Creative Writing from the University of Aberdeen. Projects include 'The Bill Gibb Line' (Aberdeen Art Gallery) and *Nevertheless* (amaBooks).

This poem lends itself well to Doric, a dialect of Scots which can't help but chime with itself. I was keen to maintain the lineation which unfolds the speaker's slow absorption of the scene, mimicking the movement of their eyes across the landscape. While the majority of the vocabulary is North-Eastern, there is a loan from Shetland in 'naver', referring both to the back of the neck and the uppermost vertebra in a sheep's neck. I also applied 'swarra' to grass, a word common to Shetland as well as the Northeast for a type of thick woollen yarn.

STEFANIE VAN DE PEER

Stefanie Van de Peer is Lecturer in Film & Media at Queen Margaret University in Edinburgh. She is originally from the north of Belgium, where Flemish (a version of Dutch) is spoken, and she loves poetry. She's been runner up in *The Times* Stephen Spender poetry in translation award in the past.

In general, translating English language poems to Dutch is straightforward—they're both Germanic languages, and Dutch is somewhere between German and English in its strictness on word order. However, the last line in the English version of this poem plays a bit with word order, so I had to be flexible, and play around a bit with possibilities. I chose to change the present tense to past participle, as I needed clarity regarding the link to the very first and the penultimate lines of the poem. 'Uitgesproken' also carries a hint of decisiveness, which I thought went well with the 'wild amen.'

Apart from that decision, there were a few instances where I was surprised to learn a new term, for example, that foxes bark. Foxes are common here in the UK, but not in Belgium, so I had to dig into the Dutch vocabulary to find out which verb to use there. Interesting!

ELISABETTA TORENO

Elisabetta Toreno is an art historian based in Glasgow. Her book on Renaissance female portraiture is due for publication in 2022.

When Chris asked me to translate this poem, I was reluctant: would I manage to convey the nurturing stillness of its wintry mood? But Chris is a persuasive kind of poet and I thank him for that—even if I cannot claim to have done enough justice to his original. A couple of technical explanations: for poetical effect 'fence-wire' in the Italian version reads as: 'wires', 'ferrous', 'of the fences'. The change also emphasises the repetition of the F fricative sound. For similar reasons, instead of 'as if', the translated version reads as 'because'.

RODERICK WATSON

Roderick Watson has written widely on modern Scottish literature. His poems feature in numerous anthologies and two main poetry collections. A new collection is forthcoming.

ROSEANNE WATT

Roseanne Watt is an award-winning writer, filmmaker and musician from Shetland. Her dual-language debut collection, *Moder Dy*, was published by Polygon in May 2019.

'Coastal Town' glossary
but—to pop up from under water ; to rise to the surface as seafowl do
djub—fisherman's word for the deep
voe—an arm of the sea
skammit—an injured surface
skoit—to look with a specific purpose
bakflan—a sudden gust of wind which, by mischance, strikes a boat's
    sail on the back side
bratwaar—broken bits of seaweed strewn along the shoreline
sheave—a slice
sair—severe

'Happens' glossary
widdi—shrubbery, small trees
daalamist—mist which gathers in the valleys at night
hömin—the early evening twilight
'dem at's awaa'—euphemism for the dead, literally: those who are away
dusts—fights, strikes
kjep—to stop a moving object
wan—past tense of 'go', also means 'one'
evalous—doubtful, uncertain, as the weather
kassen—tainted ; beginning to decay, as fish or flesh too long kept
faan upon—beginning to die, decay
blinnd—a sleep, also a dim light

sheerlin—singing, especially of birds
blue-litt—indigo

CHRISTIE WILLIAMSON

Christie Williamson is a Shetlandic poet, translator and essayist based in Glasgow. His latest publication is *Doors tae Naewye*, Luath, 2020.

Acknowledgements

Thanks are due to the editors of the following publications
and online poetry spaces in which some of these poems
first appeared:

*Causeway/Cabhsair, Dundee University Review of the Arts
(DURA), The Grantidote, The Island Review, New Writing Scotland,
Northwords Now, Poems from the Backroom, Poetry Scotland, Scotia
Extremis: Poems from the Extremes of Scotland's Psyche, Tushara.*

Some of these poems featured in 'A New Vision for Land Use in
Scotland: 6 Conversations':
https://www.seda.uk.net/land-conversations

A NOTE ON THE TYPES

Chris Powici's poems for this book are set in Palatino
Nova Pro, Hermann Zapf's & Akira Koyabashi's redesign
& updating in several weights
of Zapf's classic Palatino, which was originally
released in 1950. Renowned for its legibility,
it takes its name from Giambattista Palatino,
a calligraphy master & contemporary of Da Vinci.

Translations are set in the companion face Palatino Sans,
Zapf & Koyabashi's curved and rounded sans
serif designed as a contemporary
complement to its classic precursor.